Tendrils

Michèle Vinet

BookLand press

Published by BookLand Press
15 Allstate Parkway
Suite 600
Markham, Ontario L3R 5B4
www.booklandpress.com

Printed in Canada

Front cover image © Linjerry

Library and Archives Canada Cataloguing in Publication

Vinet, Michèle, 1946-, author
Tendrils / Michèle Vinet.

Poems.
Issued in print and electronic formats.
ISBN 978-1-77231-074-0 (softcover).--ISBN 978-1-77231-075-7 (EPUB).--ISBN 978-1-77231-076-4 (PDF)

I. Title.

PS8643.I64T46 2018 C813'.6 C2018-901638-8
C2018-901639-6

We acknowledge the support of the Government of Canada through the Canada Book Fund and the support of the Ontario Arts Council (OAC), an agency of the Government of Ontario. We also acknowledge the support of the Canada Council for the Arts, which last year invested $153 million to bring the arts to Canadians throughout the country.

I shall be telling this with a sigh
Somewhere ages and ages hence:
Two roads diverged in a wood, and I—
I took the one less traveled by,
And that has made all the difference.

~ *The Road Not Taken*
Robert Frost

Je t'écris dans la lumière.
J'ai besoin de ta lumière pour t'écrire.
La lumière du jour n'est pas la vraie lumière.

~ *La Présence pure*
Christian Bobin

Table of Contents

Driftwood

I was just driftwood
Before you
Forgotten
On forgotten beaches
And bar stools

You found me
One night
Hidden
Under the snow
Of dereliction
My hands
Like dead branches

You called me
To your talent
And held my hand
All the way back
To dignity

You cast off the layers
Of doubt and distrust
And showed me elfenfolk
Rollicking
In your blood

You brought
Apples and pears
To teach me
The taste of white
And toys
For the child
I've never been
Marbles and maps
Books and birds
And stickers for school

You gave me
Homework
Of the pictures
In my head
Laughed
And cried
And asked for more

You must have been
Thinking
About Art
That night

Your patience
Glazed and glossed
This brittle bagatelle
Into a Monet
Now perched
On the mantle
Of your courage

I was just driftwood

First Grace

The very first grace
Flashing
Wings outspread
A pale possibility
Supple as vines
On stone-dead disbelief

A moist foggy
Opal dream
Ghosting certainties
Like the promise
Of warm crusty bread
On hunger

Our biographies
Wrapped like cold hands
Around teacups
Timid crooked smiles
Smeared still
With the grimace of perdition

Our dull misery
Collecting dust
While we cowered
Behind honour and profession
And literary escape

That very first grace
Hovering
Turquoise
Like a swatch of sky
Over canyon worries
And gorge-deep fear

Tumbling
Over fuchsia infernos
Fjord distress
And apocalyptic visions
Of the end of our
Separate worlds
Proudly hand-stamped
And worn as trophies
Like hammered brass jewellery

Remember my hostility
Collapsing to mirth
To lilac drama
In the snow
Your initial patience
And curiosity
When all I scorned
I wore as black robes
Like the women of Iran

Remember your distance
Your suspicion
Of *bellissima* undress
Beneath dark veils
And guarded rubble

The first closeness
The first flight
From redolence
To safe ground
Away from you
Refusing the flowers
Of your hands
Fearful of the petals
You scattered on my wounds

Do you remember
The gentleman you
Of fortitude
Whose future was a door
Slammed
Whose sudden tenderness
Spilled
Freeing
A fresh spring
Capacity to feel

Remember the long
Slow process
Of little joys
Of water-lily innocence
And yellow-daisy delights
The furtive squirrel scurry
Of first silliness
When youth rallied around

And that first honesty
The first touch
Shy and chaste
That pulled us up
That saved us both
From drowning sure

Recall
The blast and burst
Of senses
When we pushed the world
Aside
To discover
Our rose-quarts world
Of whispers
And pink hillside

Flowerbed sighs
Our lemon-leaf
And purple-pansy
Passionworld
A fragrant foliage refuge
An uncomplicated
Straw-hat simple
Cotton-candy cloud
And pastel sunrise world

Velvet in your hands
The lavish fabric
You drape upon my past

See us as children
Swimming
Climbing
To a perched manor
Like a pirate's cove
Or treasured island
To drink champagne
And test
Again and again
Every idle bed

Chime and cherish
Rise to the glory
Of fire and flame
And mornings wan
From too much love

Mercilessness
Cannot divide us no
It loses its sting
And silver circlet tension
In the face of redemption

For luminosity declared
"At last"
Upon our chance
And late encounter

All that has gone before
Be hailed
It led us both
To us

We are a season
Opening far
As everlasting buds

Commend the dark
That gives us light
The night that wills the day

Cheer these riches
The lilt and sway
And madrigal mania
The enchantment
The beguilement
The glistening otherness
Bestowed
Upon us
In a sudden whir of grace

Felicity

I espy you
Little sweet
Felicity
Concealed
Behind his eyes
Sheltered
In his hands
Prancing silly
In his smile

I hear you
Whispering
Dizzies
And warbling jingles
In his laughter

In his name
You consign
Harmony
Thank you
And little glints
Of hooray sunniness

Both of us

Looking up
From love
You reach for
The Milky Way
With heart
So big
There's room enough
For both of us

From the doorway
You point
To constellations
You can name
And I wish
I were tall
As you
To steal them
From the sky

I travel from
Your outstretched arm
To the tip
Of your finger
And become
The falling star
You catch and clasp
To your chest

The night is cool
And once again
We dispel doubt
And turn to joy

We make the world
Too small for regrets
But big enough
For both of us

Not for too Long

Do you remember
The scent
We tried to name
Climbing to the falls

How we studied
Moss and mushroom
Wondered
At rock and crag
Breathed the lush of green
And marvelled
At the roar

I showed you caves
Where I hide
When I grieve
A niche
Never shared before

Have I told you
How very brave I've been

While you fished
Below the falls
I sunbathed
In fair undress
To show the sky
How beautiful I am
Since you

Like a piano interlude
You chuckled
At the fish you caught
And smiled them right back in
You carried lichen for me
Bringing home
The forest's cherished gifts

While others
Near about
Cried defeat
Bled their dreams
And failed at love
We exulted

We let hell run riot
Somewhere else
Then fell
Into Love's heart again
Allowing it
To close down the world
Not for too long
But long enough
For us
To build an always

Forgiveness

Can you forgive me
For not knowing you
When you were going
To ball games and parks
And drive-in movies
I don't like ball games
But I would have gone
Just to watch you cheer

Can you forgive me
For not knowing you
In high school
I would have done your homework
For the sun to kiss you more
On your bike
Or with the boys
But you might have failed Math

If I had known you
As a young man
I would have rounded up
Pretty girls for you
The beauty I never was
The little queens
Who give young men
Such giant erections

I wish I had known you
When you were driving hot rods
I would have let my hair grow
And rolled down the window
I might have worn
Bobby socks and heels
And made a felt dolly
For the rear-view mirror

But I didn't know you then
And sometimes
That makes me doubt
That kindliness exists
And has a plan
For those who wish to love
Someone
In flowerful ways

Do forgive me now
If I sometimes turn away
To catch a glimpse
Of the setting sun
The colours
Are those of my heart
Back then
When I didn't know you

I'm really sorry
About long ago
Forgive me for that
And for the way I know you now
As an answered prayer
An ocean in my lungs
And the other side of midnight
But much too late

I don't resent the fact
That your life belongs away
From our sometimes arms
And always care
Who could resent a wave
From coming in
And going out

Forgive these musings
On a playful then
On the fragility of now
Avaricious gift
Time will steal away
Leaving me to forget
Beautiful you

I hope you'll forgive me
When the day comes
I say good-bye
I love you enough to do that
You know
I love you enough
To let you go
But not without an earthquake

Promise you'll forgive me
When you're gone
And I love you still because
No sky is big enough to end you
And not even Madam Death
Has a jail so dark
That I won't see through her bars
The light of your face

Here Now

If I can't have you
Washing my hair
In heaven
I don't want to go there
What is the point
Of hell
By another name

What cruel eternity
Could piously dictate
Your hand away
From me
In sleep
Silence your voice
Or close our eyes
To each other

How could impossibly
I breathe
Know my Self
Think Beauty
Or spell Everlasting
Away from you

Gladly
I would prosecute
Any He
(Whom in His Mercy
Hath made fields
And drops of rain)
Attempting to deny
Us us

Timelessness
Begins
With you

We are here now
My heart-red you
On the outskirts
Of universal traffic
In the invisible
Seemingly seamless
Crack of time
And not even hopelessness
Has noticed

Damn all the heavens
And hells
They are fable and farce
Prayers unheard
The fears of a few
Storybook solace
With scary pictures
For the uninspired

So let's check out of time
Okay?
Let's put a sign
In the garden
Between my roses and your lilies
That dubs the house
"The Firmament"
Won't the neighbours have a fit
We'll call our street
Celestial Private
And change our names
To Immortal
And Immutable

And once and for all
Put an end to dying
As we know it
And despise it

We'll conjugate our life
In the present tense
Of the verb to Yearn
And to Be
Like the sky does
Like water
And your ice-fire fingers
On my neck

So wash my hair again
Please
I'll put lotion on your back
We'll have our timeless
And *amore* tea
Tend our flowers
Opening yesly
To the wind
And praise
This paradise
We have
All to ourselves

Yes and Faint

It roams afield
Gathering bouquets
Of intimate imaginings
My eyes behold
In its hands
My bonny self
Hitherto unknown
Perfumed
By the blooms
Whose kind and only
Cluster
Is my delight
And gratitude

Once removed from pride
Or fettered prejudice
I bend
To this tall and sudden
Generosity
Touched by petal and pistil
Dismantling strife
Building shelters
Long denied
And deemed impossible

Posies of yes and faint
Forefelt far ago
And drawn upon the margin
Of a notebook
In adolescent gloss
Dismissed and discarded then
With other hopes and dreams

I salute
This Marvel most
With florid words
For merriment

Ever before I was
Beyond scribbled worlds
Containing soul and sin
Intention prowled

Away
In meadows
Bathed in sun and shine
I unlatch
Heaven's gate
And Hell's defense

Hear
The collision
The colour fracas
On my bones
Of Certainty
Designed
Just for me

Immediate
I laugh and love
And understand
The constant stumbling
That has led
From dismay deep
Free at once and last
To wide-eyed wonder
And my belated
Secret share
Of forevers

The Art and the Story

Feather-soft phrases
Memories and mementos
Wrought
Into petal-perfect dreams

Nook and nest
Shadows for two
From porous luminance
Sepia suddenness

Brushes
Moist colour
Palette of mottled inspiration
Alizarin anticipation

A phantasy
Lays the wash
To paint a presence
On canvas fascination

The hand and breath
Are stilled
As silent medium
Appears the love

With bold strokes
Of magenta likeness
In pigment raw
Metaphor delight
And Picasso zest
We are the Art
And
We are the Story

Berries and Bananas

We sat with the sunset until
The mountain
Took it home
And when you said
Beautiful
I thought
You were talking
About night colours
On the lake

We sipped
Easy wine
And held hands
While I told stories
Of England
For your delight

I didn't know then
We would feast
On berries and bananas
At midnight
Play with the cat
And fail to turn down the covers

I didn't know
You could open doors
And asylums
With a sigh

I was unaware
Of your goodness
Then

I'm grateful
For the freckles
On your back
I've never had so many gifts
All at once

Soon
Again
I'll sit with the sunset
And improvise lore
And legends
And other jives
Just for you

A Thousand Miles

A forest
In my mind
Falls hushed
A worried dam
Bursts

Your mouth
Rescues my ruin
Drinks my disquiet
And decries
A thousand miles
Of ache

You cleanse and cool
The heat
Of brow and breast
You temper
Every flare and flame
From fire
To your kindness
Most and utter
You bring me back

Raspberry Breath

Venom violet
Knife stab
And blood-prick heart

Plaint and wail
A knot of scream
Unwound
Unfurling whip-sharp

The hunter and the hunted
Trapped in a morrow
Ever removed
From raspberry breath

Madness-rouge
Divided
By other lives
And their gadgetry

Away from warm
From embrace
The way you move
Through thickets
Of tangled arms and legs
A waste
Nibbling at o'clocks
And chronologies
Howling
To slake a thirst
Deep and liquid deeper

Heretic trenches
Scars
From battles
We have won

Wear me proudly
As the garland
Of a victor

Thirsting
For the sweat
For the craze
In your darling
For the woe
Written on the minutes
Of your hands
Or the chill
Of your departure

From poverty
And paintlessness
Blindness and discord
The protagonist turns
To folds and golds of light

Then
Sky-burst blast
Your breathlessness
And pounding heart
Such tart-smelling music

The paradox
Welcoming
Then letting go

Handsome myth
Barbed-wire dictum
Hushed by secrecy

The story of you
Unread
But by my fingers
Retold in the vibrato
The snowflake modesty
Of closeness

Crystals
Shatter on the mind
Word by verb
And phrase by still
From breath to lung
And smile to soul

Conveying you
Confusion
And lexical perplexity

Paradigm
For a paragon

Prose
Lost in the world
As hovel
And you are the Written

The Silence of the Stones

I would cheat
Never into always
If I could not touch
Your face
Or breathe you
On my pillow

I would orchestrate
Star transfusions
Dry desert alchemy
Stuff space in a glove
Endure white-azalea lunacy
To dismantle the politics
Disallowing
Our alleluia
And closed-circuit brio
Our forest-deep
And fern-scented
Aloneness

Your clutch
Candy-spice
And milk-easy
Until and beyond
The silence of the stones

To drink
Your Sauvignon kiss
To intoxication
To gorgeous poison

Planets empowered
In my mind
And I orbit
Round your name

I will the world
Still
When you open the door

A cherub
And solitude passage
Into who were are
And wish to be
And we erupt
Into bouquets
Of thanksgiving

Our former lives
Like wilted
Opera sets
Tragic
And unsung
Or wept upon
Behind the last curtain

Always is hot-immediate
Today is evernow

Hear the constellations smile
See them applaud

No Leaf so Wind

You walk through fields
Of danger
Like a stallion
On a beach
Unscathed
By dishevelment
By the highway blood
Of fast living
Or the sob of misery
Which is louder
Than the loneliness
Of the earth

Firmly
You stride
A peril path
In confidence
As if your road ahead
Were thunder

There's no taller modesty
No rain more falling
No leaf so wind
Or night so frown
As when you turn
From art
Look away from stay
And with hands
So memory
Step out of gladness
Into the fields
Again
Knowing
You may not return

Memos from Yesterday

Cool shadows
Spread evening ribbons
On the day
Blanket and drape
Havens rose-alive

Moon-cream fingers
Stroke retrospect
Into effervescence
Into unfinished kisses
As if kisses could ever end
As if love-eyes could close
And remembrance be mollified
With memos from yesterday
Pasted thick on the body
Stamp-licked on the ward
Of a sleepless mind

Crickets chant a ritual
To the ebbing of the day
While the wrist moves
Across the page
To keep alive
A citrine shine
Perfectly blaze

A marsh of indigo
Where stern he stood
A shoulderness of fern
Shadow leaves
On his face
As he searched the sky
Beyond his maple eyes

If the wonder day
Cannot be retrieved
It will not fade
Beyond her thirst
Or passed his painting heart

Regalia of words
As hand wrings pearls
From a pen
And gives necklace
And permission
To a dance and a dusk
In covert woods
Reclaimed
From felon night

Love is here ungone
And pleasure
Perched
On raven dark
Basks tiny-turtle-sunny

Scrolls are not so bold
As to unwrite
Their tale
Or make upon her hair
His Tilley never worn

Art is a bodyful experience

On a page
Of honey ink
Amorous graffiti
Spells their deliverance
And draws
Their scarlet truth

Jelly Beans

Will I one day
Outgrow
The kid
Who smiles
At the jelly beans
And gummy bears
You bring
The scaredy-cat
You coaxed
On an underwater rock
The little one
Who clasped your shoulders
Or the girl
Who skipped around you
On the beach

Will I
Dismiss ever
That small thing
That stands tower tall
In me
When you read poetry

I'll not again
Enjoy
Chocolate ice-cream cones
Like the ones
I've had with you

I don't think
I could be mature
About the way
You hold your cup
When we have tea

I'm not grown up
About the lump in my throat
Or the tear I hide
Each time you leave

But this is sure
The cheerful child
Gossamer girl
And lady porcelain
Each and all as one
Has another name
For the world

A Cruel Happiness

I love the cruel happiness
That holds us near its pain
Like a jade sea of anarchy
Keeping you away
Holding me captive
Grumbling like a revolution
As a river-rush to its destiny

Blitheness and delight
The stir of sentiment
Busy enfolding you
Being wing and flight
In a cosmos sky

Relentless riot
Making a forever vast
Out of little now
Bringing me back to want
Shining diamond-bold
In the way you move
In our restless hands

Hollow worlds dissolve
Scattering stars
And distant novas
Across our divide
Our nights alone
Our goliath and magnolia selves

I love the cruel happiness
That sets me free
From a brig called bones
Called every single day

Sometimes
I bleed lovely blue
Chasing the kiss
You send for me
From your planet far
All the way
Down the street
And up the stairs
To my universe

Prosodic thrill
In your name
In the chasm separateness
The barren land
When much too far to touch
Entwined and interlaced
Like a lofty pillar
A flawless monolith
We stumble from demands
To boundless
And prodigious us
Secretive
Illusive
Inimitable us

See the insurrection
The mutiny I become
In your absence

You
A difficult
And
Cruel happiness

Island

Downstream
From your solitude
Is an isle
A sanctuary blessed
With amity
And soft repose

No risk
To confound you
There
No brigands to abuse
Your trust
Or bind and snare
Your liberty

Only good
And gracious symmetry
A bid to verve
A kingdom blithe
And affable

Who would scorn
The choice of nature
And move
Knoll or hillock
Reef or cay
And deny
The farer
Refuge on his way

Knaves and rogues
Would dare
But far
From din and roar

You have found
A shoal
To shield your days
From malice cold
And bold dismiss

No lament
No forlorn plaint
Can now undo
Linn or loon
Strewn
Upon the flows
By the hand
Of mystic mercy
To the demise
Of those who rue
You sail
At times

Oh
The island
Loves to wait for you

It basks and boasts
And gleams
In glory found
At your approach

Laud and cheer
Every single stream
That led you once to moor

Isle and man
Have etched a course
Lost
To compasses
And maps

No One I

Suspended are the hours
Of your arms
Cathedraling
From humble chapel rest
Into stained-glass skies

Waiting for your arms
Like a lost lamb
Like a crossroad grotto
Most prayerful
And the brittle fingers
Of its Madonna

Incantations and psalms
From dawn Gregorian
To evensong vespers

The whole universe
Which is your body
Emerges
From my wish
And I sail
In its galaxy

My rain sheer skin
Pore by pore blooms
Into hymns
Of ignited nights
When open petals
Open orchid-vainer still
Gorged with dew
Upon our altar
Where fretting seraphs

Stop the skip of stars
And your song
Walks
Straight into my bones

Fair resurrection
When that forgotten
No one I
Becomes
A solemn deacon
In our ceremony

Gone yes but soon
Returning Oh
Not for how long
But for how close

A Smooth Satin Rip

Mantle your beauty
On my wounds
Gently
Entomb and inter
Faithless days
And faulty nights
With your fingers
Your bisque hands

Smile a cappella
On my silence
As a rush of wind
In greenwood grove
In dogwood copse

Sigh a word
A clement phrase
An oleander edict
Of suspended time
And pungent hush

Whisper these days
Ivory pale
Soothing
In their innocence
And wistful musings

Wash away past delinquents
Criminals and sinners
The weight of lies
Of pledges trampled
On the cobblestones
The orthography of my name

Find that moment
When visions
Erupt
Brave and bold
Upon a riddle
Called our each other
Life

Whittle a story
Of lakes
Blue deep
And luxury
Whose pools you draw
And colours you cajole
From your imagination
Into mine

Foreboding comes snaking
On the path of reverie
To bemoan
A concern
And a tedium

As I pen
Heartfelt confusions
A break occurs
On the horizon
A smooth satin rip
That hums
A little ditty

And together
From convenience we turn
To search the sky
And wonder where the other is

What dread assails
The safety of our haunt
What rusted buoy
Tracks our deepest waters
To hush the nymph
That turns our names
To canticles

Never mind the drivel
Of the fiends or the fools
They are fiction
Whose pages we can turn
To be alone again

Something immeasurable
In your eyes
Understands

The Turquoise Heart

You stood
By the window
Memorizing
The moods and fancies
Of the sky

And the blue
And the green
Of my eyes

You saved
My turquoise heart
Its gladness
Close to you

In dizzy daisies
By the falls
You learned
My lonely roots

You know
How breakable I am
In the big world

I heard you
Search my hands
In sleep
Holding dear my pulse
To feel my intravenous love
For you

You own
The purring of the cat

Her leaping joy
And kissy little paws

Forget
My impatience
At what divides us
The white lies I tell you
About hope

Keep the valleys
And the peaks
The rainbow path
That led you once
To me

Store
My elation
At your satin touch

In the palm
Of your hand
Rides my giddiness

My innocence
Leapfrogs at your footsteps
The candyfloss of your hello

Our togetherness
Your ever-love
In the gallery
Of your memory

With you
Toujours
My name by heart
My heart
By name

Oversoul

Nothing about a day
Shines so yellow
As you do

No rivulet
Ever graced a stone
As lovingly as your laughter
When it splashes
Crystal
On my times

Your fairness
Sparkles smooth
On the diamond edges
Of vocabulary

The light you write
Turns the Sun
Into suns
Into lamp posts
Painted on the sky

Sculptors
Rebuke our skill
To chisel
Marble passions
And stow them
As museum treasures
For private viewing

Crazed poets
Envy
Our rhyming names
And spend candle midnights
Imitating us

Toobadly
Unsuccessful
Let them thrash about
To no avail
Let them find
Their own oversouls

Pretty Silk

I pinned pretty silk
Flowers on my hat
To flirt with the sun
To toss in style
A wave from shore
And send it round the world
To you

An added brooch
A cat on a moon
To recognize
In mirror windows
In strangers' eyes
Or in their smiles
Only myself

Fair pansy bonnet
To make of farawayness
An idea soft and sing

My excitement
Stumbles
On the pebbles
And the shells
Of this farness

Gladly
Glockenspiel hilarity
Its hammer
On the mantra of the sea
But an ocean away
Is much too far

Continents cannot intrude
Upon the bond
That we have wrought
With tea and tenderness

I ask the sun to look away
Whilst in the shade
Of trusting palms
Surprised at purple pansies
On a blank
And virgin page
I spell a little kiss

Old World Songs

Once more
The buzz of continents
Turns my still
Into an aria

Festive cities
And glamour capitals
The architecture of the ages
Are blemished
Without you

I carve my heart
Into a pearly nautilus
Into its chambers
Where the sounds of the sea
Gently swell and sway

I have with me
Your trills and rolls
As parasol
As lyrics
In the paraphernalia
Of planes and trains

Wrap me quickly
In your music
Your sonata
Fetched from the treble clef
Of Jupiter

With tenderness
Weave for me
A cloak of eloquence
That I may return
Lustred
By bucolic landscapes
And Old World songs

See that trembling little bead
That shiver-tear
In the corner of my eye
Kiss it with a trope
Drink it with a rhyme

I'll sip sherry or Madeira
I'll say your name
A thousand times a day
Since you are my home

Foreign Fever

Softly
From passed remembrances
And other latitudes
To salty skies
The white
And blazing light
Of pink laurels
And mimosa gold

Girls on the beach
Burnished angels
Bronze-beautiful
And hot

Goddesses
Maple toffee queens
With jewelled navels
And silver nipples
Riding the lust of men
Their masculine submission
With naked daring
Caramel cunning
And roasted almond-cream poise

Wine and whiskey reasons
For reminiscing
For letting then and when
Colour and shape this escapade
Mellowed by the navy sea
And stir of palms

Ochre earthen sigh
And deep-night blues
A flush of senses

Coastal heat
And vines
Sweetening the easy
Humming balcony
Where you nestle
Hard on my mind

Wait for me
I'll be back soon
In Quixote frenzy
Monaco elegant
And Riviera warm

On my eyes
You'll taste the amber
Bodies of the shore
The foam and crash
Of wander waves

I'll bring you France
And set it on our bed
With wine
And bread
To make of coming home
A gift of foreign fever

Epiphanies

Fantasies
In the rain

Drizzle
On my eyes
In my mouth
Wet and tasty

On my skin
A seizure
Deep as marrow
Close as epiphanies

Your rainy
Giant solitude
That most miracle
Of miracles

All day rain
On the arid fields
Of my quotidian

Thirsting roots
Drink all of you
They can
In case
Parched dreams
Fail
To find again
Sufficient strength to thrive

Spin and Shine and Sheen

I need rescue
From a thing
So old as
Gimme

I stand straight and tall
At your melody ode
And singful say

A little fear so
Big is made
A bigger far can hurt

But love
My you
My clear and free
Your flower arms
And never no
Ocean-mountain me

Some slice a wave
To watch it bleed
A bird would fly but for a cap
Failure grows a limb
Then hobbles on a cane

I bare a smile
To let a whine and wail
Unharm a thought
Of biggest you

Rampant chaos
As trade and fare

Lost and found
We'll turn our backs
On lightlessness
And we'll make spin
And shine and sheen

Open wide
Your cosmos heart
Let me enter fast
Its mischief grin

Your love
As cordial riddle
And enigma

Fluorescent Dusk

I wish
I could capture
Samba sunsets
By the lake
To bring them back to you
In sheaves

I could list the colours
But you would fail to see
The red of rays
The evanescent riches
Of each fluorescent dusk

But we are
Close as bark and trunk
Green and grass
Heart and bleed
Close as book to page
And word to meaning

When I fall into your arms
You will feel my suns
Warm and summer green
And impishly proud

You will see
And you will hear
Every
Water wind
And moonly sun
I have saved for you

Bring misty rainbows
In your hands
And I'll bring sunsets
In my eyes
So we can have
Our own private sky

Still and Star

I'm coming home
From summer
With its face
Of gold upon mine

I'm coming back
From water
With sapphire
On my mind

I'm leaving
Still and star
For city streets
And sidewalk shuffle

I have toiled
Over lore and myth
For you
And written
Dungeons dank
And batty belfries
Thesauruses
And glossaries

From tree and shrub
And rhubarb silly
I've gathered leaves
Enough
For opuscules
And opuses

I'll miss the quiet
But every bag and case
Brings me
Near to you

Knowing
You live and breathe
Close by
Is all I need
To feed my whim
And my semantics

I've packed my dulcet suns
And books
To make of snow
A picnic tablecloth
When I get cold again

Tropics

I have lots of socks
Embroidered
With pretty flowers
Cosy woollies too
But I wear yours
To have something
Of you on me

I wear them
Like emblems
Unafraid
To dance with you
Down my waltz
To truths
And certainties

Your funny socks
Spill
About my ankles
Warm a bracelet there
Then fall
To wrinkles
Of merriment

With your socks
There is no winter now
No desolation
I cannot cross

See my sureness of foot
The tropics where I frolic
See how I sally forth
Wearing you

A Patria Kind

Somewhere I never became
The matronly figure
Greeted
By passers and friends
The stranger in my room
Whose presence
I fail to know

Somehow I ever remained
A girl
Curious and shy
For whom the sun
Was a pretty
And all else a ploy
To bend the heart
To earth
Its folly
And its fury

Sometimes always
I wonder if
In the safety you provide
For my play
You see
Who fills these bones
Of misfortune
What makes this pilgrim
Plod ahead

You ever someday looked at me
Your goodness as a land
A country of respite
A seaport
And permission
To otherness and otherwheres

Someone is that only
Space
Where I bloom again
Without thorns
For your pleasure mauve
And meditation

Someplace always
I invent
To survive and feast
On the breathing of the roses
Their perfume deliberate
A patria kind
Where I never become
The one you did not find
But am remembered
And restored
As the missing part of you

You welcome the exception
That somewhere never
I became
But think me perfectly sky
And beautiful

From Far and Fear

In that part of me
Remaining hushed
But alert
A spool of silk unfurls
Threads and webs
Searching the glossary
Of stars
For meaning

Above every if
And each perhaps
It asks and calls
For you
While ashen moons
Waste away
Throttled and bewildered
By the shiver
Of a winter's gasp

Wound around
The litany of the poor
Loves relinquished
And wars and deaths
My questions bray
Like Spanish mules

Bursts of flame
Fuel my quest
My changeless need
My dream of you
With a coterie
Of beasts and diablos
Holding council

Lazy sun-tears
Spark the discourse
The monsters weep
And brawl and fuss
And intone
Oratorios of despair

From their wasteland
Like occult priests
Strands of hope
Work their magic
Into vanity and belief

My incantations
And witchery
Have brought you back
From far and fear
From Madam Destiny's
Decrees

To hear you
Opening the door
To see your smile
Run up the stairs
To hear my name
As Hosanna
I wait I wait

Sleep dispels frivolity
And from its sovereign throne
My loneliness
Brandishes its sceptre
Its mighty sword
Plunges once again
Through the tapestry
Of my chimera

Still
I wait I wait

Artistry

The whir of the work
Keeps you busy
Rushing tasks
Culprit time-cult
Setting the pace
Dictating thought
Slaying the possible
Caterwauling demands
And salt sweat

Welcome to Everyday
For Everyman
Work as
Pillage
Achievement or abdication

This day
Labour as static
Parasitic drone in the senses
Cheap recovery from yesterdays
Demeaning and disparaging

You withdraw
Guitarfish
Hiding in the berries
Of gulfweed

A sudden foolish fancy
Imperceptible
Foliate follies
Ignoring the foofaraw
Of chain of command

Survival trade-off
In full-moon bliss
At midday
Broad daylight arrogance
Consolation of the wounded
And betrayed

Emeralds and rubies
From the other side
Of wants and whims
In your aura
Candlelight piano
Soothing like a remedy
Like a country-wagon elixir
For modern heartache

Your pulse
On the Richter scale
Your hand to your ear
Maestro conch fitting
For lily glee
Rhododendron petal-sounds
Winged and moist
Flute flutter
And glass-feather frailty
Magnolia-scented hyphen
Hypnotic tremolo
Between life and Life

Concert sensations
Organza kiss
Concubinage of hemp
And lustrous taffeta
Your mind as tapestry

Cadenza and rest
You

The notes on the staff
Her name
The time signature

Comes the plea
In a major key
Molto ritardando
Let there be no end
To luxuria
Here you listen
And allow the escape
To drum
In perpetuum

Sensual sparks
Destiny and defiant fist
On the jaw of immortality
On a planet gone to odium
And guns
And blood

But this for you
Incomparable artistry
On a workday
Inspiration bold and blatant
On the shambles
Of the ordinary

Craftsmanship
Subliminal euphoria
Subverting neon numbing
Fountainhead of power
In a disfigured world
Reverie
To hear again and again
At will
The touch of a lady

Wednesdays

Panorama
Technicolour soulscape
The spelling
And the grammar
Of a purpose

Chromium dreams
On your body
My name
For your solace
Cashmere cozy
And Christmas kind

Apart
We are homesick
Out of place
Suspicious hoodlums
In a jail
Called other lives
But together
The glissando
The yellow freedom
Of the hour

The mirage
Pleads and prays
And drinks
A flagon
Of Italian
Cooked wine
Sweet and strong

Looms always
Mahogany scintilla
In your eyes
Plankton flavours
On your lips

The signal is now given
Our preference rings
Vibrant luscious rampage

The obvious
And essential dilemma
We are us
And you are not
Me without you
And who is left behind

Another day
Is just a date
And an undoing
Bleeding
Moribund memories
Blue and ballistic

Jealous calendar ransom
Bargains and conclaves
To negotiate the night
Entice Madam Dusk
And other bothers
To spill incense
On our longing
Liberal license
Like gillyflower fields

Take me back to madness
To our exclusive
Hysteria
When we voyage
Far
Out of reach and reason
Into Wednesdays

Alphabets of Leaf

I whisper
Your name
To the moon
Perched high
On a pine

I murmur it
To the lake
Blinded by night

I listen
For an echo
And the wind
Rustles and sifts
Through alphabets of leaf
Then rests at my feet

On the road you trod
I call you
Sleepy milkweed shiver
And blush
Remembering
Your passage

Water bouquets
Stand still
As I breathe
Your name
Then faint
In their own perfume

I hum it then
And a thing
Bigger than fast
But smaller than hurt
Trembles
In the air

I whistle
Your name
And morning breaks
So loud
And more than stars
That I am lifted
Harp and heart
Dew and damp
Sun and rise
To the face of joy

Upon the Page

I lay you down
On paper
The same way
I lay you down
Upon my life
Of lucky breaks
And glass-shard faith
With sincerity
And quiet deliberation

I write you
With the same integrity
I reveal
Within my silence
Beneath my silks
When yonder world
Has gone away
And we exult
At being born
Of each other

I spell your name
Upon the page
The same way I say it
To touch the sound it makes
In the air
And the trace it leaves
Upon my history
Upon my way of walking
Straight into its culture
And amnesty

I draw upon the page
Innumerable stars
Dimmed and doomed
By the dawn
When you spoon me to you
From that far frontier
Called the edge of the bed

Months go Apriling
Over my page
When you build moons and morns
From dark and night and never

Like Jacks and Jills
In cartwheels and somersaults
My fears go tumbling down
The hill

Around the corner
From every word
As far as heart can reach
And pencil race
You happen
Unconditionally

From the surface of my skin
To the *vibrato forte*
Of my blood
You occur

Tendrils
Round my bones
Round my lonely way
Of drifting
Into you

No exclamation mark
Can wonder at your hand
In my hair
No question mark
Knows if you will stay

There are no birds
Or feathers rife enough
To quill and quell
The lexicon
Writing love
On our lives

In bright black robes
Madam Death

Briefings from Eternity

Mountain sorrow
Peaked and cold
Marble blue
And midnight dark

A saline wound
That does not heal
A war I lose
Every day

To be a lighthouse
To guide you home
On a skyless eve
And fury sea

Clawing at the afterlife
For posts and cards
And briefings
From eternity

The Apples and the Cellos

I wear your death
Like a wedding gown
Like a nuptial vow
An apprenticeship
In heartbreak and regret

I wear your dying
The way I wear your ring
Like the circle of the moon
Round and pregnant
Strewn with ash

Lyrical solitude
The apples and the cellos
Of your love
As ambrosia and resonance
Your stark finale
In my symphony
And resurrection

My lavish sorrow
Drags heavy wings
Across measureless
Hells
Plumes and pinions
Albatross aloft

I miss
Your minstrel way
Of singing my hands
Into yours

Odes and ballads
A romance medieval
Or two or four
As a way of making do
Of the world without you

Tears as oceans
On that continent
My life
The earth on which you loved
And lived

Return to my story
That my black
Be nothing more
Than spilled ink
A blemished paragraph
On a soiled page

I wish you
Again alive
And alove

I'll gorge on my pages
And I'll drink them
Until I am the Book
Of You

The Pink and the Petals

Sombre wizardry
Prison walls
Burden days
And discontent

Waiting
For the ruffle
Of the wings
Of the chickadees

For the pink
And the petals
Of a blush and a kiss
On my fancy

Helpless
Like a bird
On a branch
On a day
When the sky
Just won't breathe

Waiting with ferns
And festivals
Oranges
And boysenberries

Waiting with tulips
With bijou ornaments
For the waltz
For the foxtrot

Clinging to myths
And the silver flight
Of a smoky phoenix
Or glossy griffin

The once again
Of thrill and thrum
Of things last
And last things

Expecting
Death to apologize
And wail and thrash
With chagrin
And bring you back

To me

Fallow Soul

Saying goodbye
From the cobalt shock
The convulsion
In my lungs

In our garden
Irate roses
Hide their face
And sob

A glass of wine
On the porch
To slake
My fallow soul

Gone
The glory
Shared with no one
Saved for none

Lost passages
I traveled near
So breathing close to you
Gods were palpable

Slumber I never nearly know
Since your life
Is boreal
And dust flung far

Snows and summers
Nevermindly
Pass over and around
And storms and passions
Happen far away

Tornadoes of the heart
That always never
Say never
Only soon

A bigness called *l'amour*
Sunflowerful
Comes running in
Tripping over yellows
Of nostalgia
Ceruleans of grief

To ease the pain
Leaf and branch and tree
Bedeck the memories
With bouquets
Wine and books

A new scenario
And annotated script

So no
Not goodbye
But little sweet hellos
Hopping happy
On my shoulders

Are you that purple star coming out?

The Last Dance

You walk into my senses
As if throwing open
The glass doors
Of a Versailles ballroom

Your light
Guilds my palest mien
And sudden liquid gold
Floods my veins

Something in your stride
Derides the earth
And gambols on the world
Like a trampoline child

A livened bond
Stirs in my revelry
Sentinels of thoughts
Scurry fast to greet you

The winter in my mind
Dreams of seashine lush
Wastelands play hopscotch
On my fire

Nearer you tread
Greater the shoot of star
Centuries fall in my hands
You are still so far

Your eyes throw bridges
On infinity
Lest I too perish
Before you kiss me once again

Green and scaly dragons
Bristling in my anger
Stop their spit and stomp
And scream and singe

You flit and hover close
A ghost and spirit shepherd
A beauty butterfly
Kissing my ceaseless pain

You touch me then
And my love wild and heart
Dreams and glows and cries
To welcome you close

In its silk tuxedo
Your heart takes a final bow